IMAGES
of England

IN AND AROUND
ROTHERHAM

FROM THE SCRIVENS COLLECTION

Station Row, Laughton Common.

College Square, Rotherham.

IMAGES
of England

IN AND AROUND
ROTHERHAM
FROM THE SCRIVENS COLLECTION

Compiled by
Peter Tuffrey

TEMPUS

Tempus Publishing Limited
The Mill, Brimscombe Port,
Stroud, Gloucestershire, GL5 2QG

ISBN 0 7524 1104 7

Typesetting and origination by
Tempus Publishing Limited
Printed in Great Britain by
Midway Clark Printing, Wiltshire

This book is dedicated to Geoff Thomas – thanks for your help once again.

Wentworth Woodhouse, from the gardens.

Contents

Acknowledgements

I would like to thank the following people for their help:
Paul Fox, Tony Munford and his staff in the Local Studies and Archives Section at Rotherham Library, Geoff Thomas. Gratitude should also be expressed to Rotherham Libraries for allowing a number of their pictures to be reproduced here.

The photographer, Mr Edgar, Leonard Scrivens.

Introduction

In 1996, I produced a book of Edgar Leonard Scrivens' photographs of Doncaster. Now, three years later, I am pleased to offer another book of his pictures – In and Around Rotherham, and who knows there may be more volumes, illustrating other areas that he covered, in the future.

During the autumn of 1985, I travelled south to meet Scrivens' only surviving daughter, Ivy. She told me that her father was born in 1883, and first became interested in photography when he was at school, obtaining his first camera whilst still a pupil. In time he worked as a press photographer, establishing a photographic business in Cooper Street, Doncaster, during the first decade of the twentieth century. Other companies in Doncaster at this time included Don Lion, Arjay Productions Empire Views, Regina Company Press, and J. Simmonton & Son. All these companies produced picture postcards, but Scrivens was to become the leading exponent of this trade, not only in his own town but, arguably throughout South Yorkshire too. This is because, for the next thirty years, he captured on his postcards, almost every main road, street or thoroughfare in nearly every town and village within a forty mile radius of Doncaster. He also took pictures in Derbyshire, Whitby and York.

All Scrivens' postcards bear his unmistakeable initials E.L.S, and he evolved a meticulous numbering system for his cards. On a card numbered 172-27, the first number denotes the locality, in this case number 172 relates to Rotherham. The second number indicates that the postcard is the 27th in the Rotherham series. Scrivens photographed over 250 localities, with a fair number of cards in each series.

Over the years, Scrivens' postcards have grown in popularity, reflected in the prices paid for them by dealers and collectors. His pictures show scenes prior to industrial, commercial or road way developments and this is what makes the pictures in this book particularly interesting. In his views of Bridgegate, Rotherham, we see the thoroughfare before and after widening. We see Anston and Wickersley before the advent of the motor car and subsequent roadway developments. He has also not only photographed the former rural splendour of some villages, but recorded their evolution into sprawling mining communities which is unique in an area like Rotherham. We see this evolution in the views of Dinnington and Maltby.

Scrivens postcard views have outstanding clarity, are beautifully composed and full of incidental detail and curious features. An example of the latter is evident in the view of Market Place, Rotherham, where the Tramway's Department's track cleaner is visible. Additionally, he always seems to have been able to persuade an army of children to pose in his views, adding charm and interest to the scene.

During the 1920s and 1930s, Scrivens re-photographed a number of locations, already recorded earlier in his career, adding the letter 'G' or 'V', depending on the period, to the numbering on the cards. We see this practice clearly in the views of the Bridge Inn and College Street, Rotherham.

By the 1920s, Scrivens had moved his photographic business to Queen's Road, Doncaster, whilst living with his wife and two daughters in Craithie Road, Doncaster. At this time, his postcard and developing/printing business flourished. His postcard views were sold in a variety of outlets including newsagents and stationers. Scrivens' daughter Ivy remembers that the Queen's Road premises were methodically organized to accommodate the various photographic processes, with up to twenty-five people being employed to cope with the workload. She also recalls that her father rarely brooded on matters and often arrived home in the evenings whistling 'Tip-toe Through the Tulips'. He had virtually no other interests apart from photography and frequently lectured on the subject to local camera clubs and other photographic societies.

When Scrivens died in 1950 and his business was sold, no one bothered to save the thousands of postcard view negatives neatly filed in pigeon holes in an upstairs room at Queens Road. Nobody appreciated their worth or could ever have envisaged that Scrivens would come to be known as one of the region's major topographical artists. At one time, there was a strong local rumour that a subsequent owner of the Queen's Road premises dumped the glass plate negatives in a hole on the site and covered them with concrete. However, having contacted the person myself who was said to have done this, the allegation was strenuously denied!

Peter Tuffrey
April 2000

One

Rotherham
The Villages

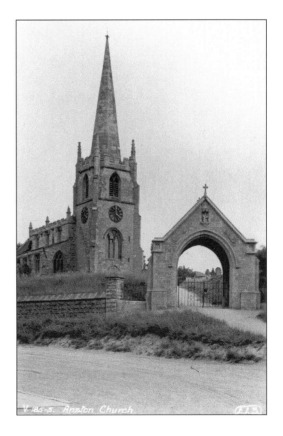

The church of St James at Anston, is an ancient building of stone, erected about 1150, but chiefly in the Early English style. The reredos erected in 1900, was a memorial to Mrs Roberts, relict of the late Samuel Roberts of Sheffield, a generous benefactor to the church. An organ was provided in 1899. The nave and chancel were restored in 1886 and the aisles and porch in 1890. There were 300 sittings. A lych-gate was built as a war memorial around 1920 and cost around £1,000.

Bawtry Road or Bramley Hill, facing east, with the old Ball Inn visible in the distance. Interestingly, the *Rotherham Advertiser* (23 April 1949) notes, 'Bramley occupies a proud place in the world of Methodism.' In 1786, John Wesley preached in the Methodist church there, afterwards lunching with General Spencer, a well-known local landowner of the period. The church had been opened the previous year by the Revd Joseph Benson. Copies of the text used by both speakers have been typed and affixed on the underside of the stool from which Wesley preached, which is still present at Bramley.

According to the Rotherham Rural District Council By-Law Building Plans 1897-1947, the first plans for housing in Cross Street, (stated as being Ball Lane) Bramley, were submitted in 1905. This was for the development of a number of properties by Waddington, Francis and Balby. The view here shows Cross Street looking north, with the Ball Inn, rebuilt around 1912, on the right.

Flanderwell (not Flanders as mentioned on the postcard view) Avenue, Bramley. The village, lying east of Rotherham, has been noted as retaining its rural charm until well into the twentieth century.

Main Street, Bramley, with photographer Edgar Leonard Scrivens' motor vehicle included in the picture on the left. It is noted in *Rambles In Ivanhoe Land*, H. Wild, undated, 'The village of Bramley, which lays away from the High Road, with the exception of a few cottages and the two inns the Ball and the Travellers' Inn, is a pleasant walk from Rotherham, the four mile stone stands at the roadside just before one enters the village near the lodge of Bramley Park.'

E.L.S.209-8. The Grange, Bramley.

H. Wild also states, 'Bramley Grange...in former days was a Grange of the Abbots of Roche [Abbey]...only one end can have any claim on being the original monastic building, the following restoration dates, 1639, 1716 and 1755 appearing in various parts of the house. When, after the dissolution of the monasteries, their [the Abbotts] wealth and belongings were parcelled out, Bramley Grange, for a century or two was in the hands of the Spencers [for nearly 300 years].'

E.L.S.209-13. Wesleyan Chapel, Bramley.

Bramley Methodist chapel was erected in 1785 for Mathew Waterhouse. The building bears the inscription: 'John Wesley preached here July 1st 1786'. The building was converted to a private dwelling around 1975.

5.163-4. Laughton Road, Dinnington.

Dinnington Palace cinema/theatre was built around 1915 by James England and some local businessmen. The building was eventually converted to a supermarket. Allan Harvey, in *Palace Cinema* (1980) recalls that the establishment of the cinema was a great step forward for the area and a real money-spinner. For the first year of the Palace there was a break in the film's programme for a 'live' stage show. Full houses were usual and the best seats had to be reserved. The film's programme consisted of Pathe's Gazette, the serial, the main feature and a comic to finish. Off-centre to the right, is the Lyric theatre, built in 1910, James England being the main instigator. England's son Fergus was involved in much of the construction work. Two flats were contained above the entrance and there were two down below. Allan Harvey notes that the actors who came to the Lyric and the Palace usually lodged in New Street, then a very respectable area. He also adds, 'The Lyric had prosperous and lean years.' At one time it was a Salvation Army Citadel, though during the Second World War it had a revival and was a popular venue for dancing. The Lyric, was bought by the local Parish Council in 1962, for £1,800.

The church of St Leonard, at Dinnington, was rebuilt in 1868 at the expense of John Carver Athorpe. It is a building of limestone, in the Gothic style, its features including a turret containing one bell. Several stained windows in the church are to the memory of various members of the Athorpe family. The church was enlarged in 1906, by the erection of a new north aisle, the extension of the nave and the addition of vestries. In 1911, the chancel was rebuilt and extended and new choir stalls added as a memorial to the late Revd G.M. Athorpe, rector 1870-1882, at a total cost of around £900. There were about 350 sittings.

Scene in Laughton Road, Dinnington. During the 1920s, it was claimed that all the streets in Dinnington were well lit by gas supplied by the Dinnington Gas Company, which also provided the needs of those requiring light and heat for domestic purposes. Allegedly, the 'gas was good and the price exceptionally low.'

14

E.L.S. 183-12. The Hall, Dinnington.

It is claimed that the original Dinnington House/Hall was built by Henry Athorpe in 1756. In time he was succeeded by his nephew Robert Athorpe, who made the house more imposing. The house was later purchased from the Athorpe family by the National Coal Board.

E.L.S 183-25. A Bit of Old Dinnington.

A little bit of old Dinnington.

Doe Quarry Lane, Dinnington. In 1900, Dinnington's population was 285. By the Second World War, it was about 7,500. Up to 1900, there were just a few farms, the old inn and a small methodist chapel. The sinking of the colliery changed all that, turning a small hamlet into a village of urban dimensions.

View of Lorden's Hill, Dinnington. In the Dinnington 1937 Coronation souvenir edited by Herbert Frith it is stated that, 'There are streets of splendid shops, well equipped for serving the community; banks and post offices; cinema; concert hall, which give a town-like appearance to the village.' By 1950, it was recorded that Dinnington had 112 shops – a total which gave the area one shop for every 70 people – an average higher than Rotherham or Worksop. The commercial premises, fronting the building in the picture, have since been converted to a private dwelling.

16

183-6. Dinnington Colliery. Copyright Scrive

Two pictures of Dinnington colliery, one of five collieries owned by the Amalgamated Denaby Collieries Ltd, comprising Denaby, Cadeby, Maltby, Rossington and Dinnington. The sinking of the shafts at Dinnington started in September 1902 and then March 1903, with the Barnsley seam reached in February 1904 and February 1905 respectively. Coke ovens were attached to the colliery in 1907. Also, adjacent, was a brickyard, producing good, sound engineering bricks. By the late 1930s, it was recorded that the colliery owned 715 houses in the village and found employment for a gross total of approximately 1,700 men and boys. A set of pithead baths was installed in 1937 for the workmen.

E.L.S. 183-21. Dinnington Colliery.

Dinnington's *Official Guide* around 1925 states that the Colliery Institute, 'is the chief centre [of recreation] and home of sport and pastimes of every description - indoor and outdoor. Its large and handsomely furnished billiard room contains six first-class tables. It houses a large concert hall, library, reading room, card rooms etc. Here are to be found the headquarters of the various sections of sport. The grounds of the institute are laid out for football, cricket, bowling, tennis etc. and are considered to be amongst the best in the region. The Yorkshire County Cricket team have been entertained there on several occasions, on one of which – be it never forgotten – Dinnington almost won.'

The Bandstand, Coronation Park, Dinnington.

The Lodge, Firbeck Hall.

E.L.S. 63-15. Firbeck Hall.

Commenting on Firbeck Hall in 1828, historian Joseph Hunter said, 'An old Elizabethan fabric, but when in [Henry Gallyknight's hands] has been made to fall in with views of modern convenience and elegance.' From this, it was assumed that Henry extended the hall, and to quote historian Sir Nicholas Pevsner, 'Elizabethanised it by the addition of steep gables.' During the remainder of the nineteenth century, the hall had several owners including, a Mrs Miles of Bristol, and the Revd Henry Gladwyn Jebb. In 1914, the building was the home for several Belgian families. Around 1934, Cyril Nicholson acquired the premises and converted them into a country club. Later, the building became an annex for the Sheffield Royal Infirmary.

Interestingly, Norman Hill, in the *Postal History of Rotherham & District* (1960), mentions that the Firbeck mails were first carried by rural letter-carrier (foot-post, postman) from Tickhill. A wall box was opened on 4 November 1870. The post office, under Rotherham, opened on 3 May 1890, with Mary Elizabeth Ward as sub-post mistress. Telegraph business commenced on 25 July 1893.

Firbeck's church of St Peter is a small edifice of stone in the Norman style, consisting of chancel, nave, north aisle, south porch and tower at the north-west angle, erected in 1900 at the expense of Mrs Jebb. This was built in memory of Revd Henry Gladwyn Jebb of Firbeck Hall (d.1898), and contained eight tubular bells. The church was thoroughly restored in 1887, when it was re-seated, re-roofed and a new organ was added. There were 2,880 sittings and the register is said to date from 1721.

The *South Yorkshire Times*, of 19 August 1916, announced that sinking operations at the Firbeck Colliery, Langold, had begun. The *Rotherham Advertiser*, of 16 May 1925, noted that the Barnsley seam was reached at a depth of 826 yards.

Firbeck is situated ten miles east of Rotherham, and the population at the time the picture was taken around 1920, was 203. The residents involved with commerce, included grocers, farmers, market-gardeners and joiners.

Street scene at Firbeck. S.G. Jebb Esq. JP, who once owned the manorial rights, and Lt-Col. Henry Kenyon Stephenson of Sheffield, were formerly the only landowners in Firbeck.

Main Street, Greasbrough, with cycle agent and general dealer G. Elliott's business premises on the right

Potters Hill, Greasbrough. Scrooby Street is to the left, along with the Prince of Wales public house, the license dating from 1868.

E.L.S. 222-15. Church Street, Greasbrough.

Church Street, Greasbrough. Greasbrough village is two miles north of Rotherham and its township once included the neighbouring hamlets of Basingthorpe, Ginhouse, Nether Haugh and part of Parkgate. A Local Board was established in 1873, but this was superseded by an Urban District Council of twelve members formed under the Local Government Act of 1894.

G. 222-3. Church Street, Greasbrough. Copyright.

Church Street, Greasbrough, with the War Memorial on the right. At one time there were four methodist chapels in Greasbrough: the United Methodist Free Church was built in 1854; the Congregational Chapel in 1874; the Primitive Methodist in 1880, and the Wesleyan Chapel in 1893.

222-20. Potters Hill, Greasbrough.

Potters Hill, Greasbrough. The population of Greasbrough during the early 1920s was just over 3,000, and in the ecclesiastical parish was 2,665. The area of the township and Urban District comprised of 2,413 acres, of which 2,376 were land and 37 water. Earl Fitzwilliam was formerly the principal landowner.

Toll Bar Lane, Greasbrough.

Looking down Union Street, Harthill, towards Serlby Lane. It has been said that the period 1901-1937, saw the beginning of great changes in Harthill, 'The old, dusty limestone roads were gradually macadamised, the wagonette and gig gradually disappeared, and the telephone and telegraph disappeared...' The single-storey building on the left was, for many years, a sweet shop occupied by a Miss Featherstone.

Greasbrough, with the parish church of St Mary's in the distance. The foundation stone for the structure, designed in the Gothic style by Charles Watson and J.P. Pritchett, was laid on 29 September 1826, by Viscount Milton. The church was consecrated in 1828. C. Wilson in *Greasbrough - A History*, explains that with the village's population rising during the first quarter of the nineteenth century, the old chapel of ease – The Chapel of Holy Trinity - was inadequate for the number of Anglican people residing there. Earl Fitzwilliam and the people of Greasbrough provided a site for the new church. It was adjacent to the old chapel which was demolished.

Union Street, Harthill, with the Square and Compass public house on the right, and All Hallows church in the distance. *Harthill with Woodhall* (1989) mentions that there has been a church on this site for at least 900 years. It is thought that a church was built in 1085 and was dedicated to St John the Baptist. The present dedication to All Hallows came sometime before the nineteenth century. Very little now remains of the Norman church.

Blue Bell public house, Harthill. The photograph was taken at a time when Joseph Webster was noted as the 'licensed retailer of beer and spirituous liquors.' Garbett, in *Harthill and Woodhall* (1950), records that the pub, demolished and rebuilt in 1923, had a fine old malt kiln at the rear, and was the home of a branch of the Glossop family from around 1690 to 1830.

Bridge Street, Killarmarsh.

E.L.S. 223-2. The Vicarage, Hooton Roberts.

The Vicarage, Hooton Roberts. The village is situated on the main road from Rotherham to Doncaster, and many of the properties that make up the community are situated along it. At one time, Earl Fitzwilliam was Lord of the Manor and sole landowner in the area. The origin of the place name is suggested by Nora Sleath, in *The Story of Hooton Roberts* (1965), 'In Domesday, Hotun. Tun means a homestead. The church, anciently known as St Peter's, was built around 1100 by Robert de Hoton, The latter's son, Sir William, succeeded him in about 1130, but the village did not bear its name until 1285, when another Robert de Hoton, to distinguish it from its neighbours Hooton Levitt, and Hooton Pagnell, added his own name. This Robert seems to be the last of the de Hotons.' At the beginning of the twentieth century, Hooton Robert's main commercial occupants were farmers. Other people listed included, a gamekeeper, a quarry owner, and Elizabeth Wilson who was the shopkeeper and postmistress. The population of Hooton Roberts at the time the picture was taken around 1910, was 245.

N. Pevsner in *Derbyshire* (1953) says that the interest in Killarmarsh's church of St Giles is 'the Norman doorway (one order of colonnettes, capitals with leaves, arch with zig zag in intrados and extrados). The Late Perps window should also be noted in which all curved forms of Gothic arches have gone straight.'

Rotherham Corporation, tramcar No. 14, is pictured at Kimberworth. In Kimberworth *Manor, Township and Parish*, C. Wilson (1988), it is said that Kimberworth is more than a village on a hill. It has been an ancient manor since Anglo-Saxons lived there a thousand years ago. It was a separate township from 1756 until its combination with Rotherham when the County Borough was created in 1871, and it has been an ecclesiastical parish since 1841.

Two views of the Manor, Kimberworth. A datestone on the front of the building bears the date, 1694. In the picture below, a dovecote from the seventeenth/eighteenth century can be seen in the foreground.

Jordan Locks, Kimberworth.

Kimberworth Wesleyan chapel, at the junction of Kimberworth Road and Psalters Lane. Behind the building is the Kimberworth Trinity church.

V 184-11. Laughton Church.   Scrivens.

The church of All Saints at Laughton, is a building of limestone principally in the Early Perpendicular style, being the third church on the same site. It consists of chancel, nave aisles, south porch and an embattled western tower with pinnacle and spire rising to a height of 185 feet. The church contains a remarkable doorway belonging to the first Saxon church. There is a monument to the Eyre family, dated 1619, another to that of Hatfield (long term residents at Laughton) and two kneeling figures of Richard and his wife, of New Hall Grange, dated 1605. The first church dates from around 1200; the church was restored in 1896 and afforded 500 sittings. To the west of the church is the site of Earl Edwin's Castle.

E.L.S. 184-4. Interior, Laughton Church.

An old gateway, Laughton.

E.L.S 184-8. An Old Gateway, Laughton.

E.L.S. 184-6. High Street, Laughton

High Street, Laughton. The population in 1901, was 631 in the township and 926 in the ecclesiastical parish. At one time in the village, there was a police station of the West Riding Constabulary with one constable, and two cells.

Firbeck Lane, Laughton. There was an increase in Laughton's population from 1901-1931. One of the reasons for this occurred in 1904, when the South Yorkshire Joint Railway was built, bringing railway workers to the area.

C.W. Wright in *The Character of Laughton-en-le-Morthen* (1967), says the curiosity of newcomers to the village must immediately be aroused by the stark contrast between the old village of Laughton and the nearby red-brick colliery villages. 'Although Laughton lies in the official green belt of Rotherham and Sheffield, it is surrounded by its own green belt of agricultural land into which the colliery villages have not been allowed to intrude.'

Street scene, Letwell. It is claimed that in Norman times, the land that is now Letwell, belonged to Tickhill Castle and was first cleared out of the forest for farming purposes.

Scrivens, has captured a lively scene at Station Row, Laughton Common. The sinking of the Maltby, Dinnington and Firbeck Collieries led to a further increase in Laughton's population.

The three-storeyed Letwell rectory was built in the eighteenth century, for a yeoman farmer, and features mullioned windows. A brass quote on the doorstep reads, 'Peace and grace be to this place.'

It is suggested that Letwell may have acquired its name from all the wells in the vicinity, whilst piped water was first brought into the village in 1935, at a cost of £25,000. Main sewers were laid in the late 1940s, until then earth closets had been used.

S. 43-41. Maltby Colliery.

The sinking of Maltby Main began in 1908, and the task was not without several mishaps. On 31 March 1909, three men were killed, and on 19 August of the same year, a man was fatally injured falling down the shaft. On 17 June 1910, the sinkers' efforts were rewarded, a rich seam of the Barnsley bed being struck at a depth of 820 yards.

E.L.S. 43-74. Garden Front, Hooton Levitt Hall.

The garden front, Hooton Levitt Hall, Maltby.

The Don Jon public house at Maltby. The area remained quite a small place until the twentieth century. The population in 1811 was only 602, and it had reached no more than 716 by the 1901 census. However, within the next 10 years, the colliery had started production, as had the local brickworks, and the population had more than doubled to 1,750.

The Well, Maltby.

North Anston's panoramic view.

North Anston, seen here from the South Anston end of Ryton Road, with the area up to the railway embankment undergoing much redevelopment in the intervening years. The new A57 road now bypasses the village. The area where the steam lorry can be seen is dissected by Anston crossroads, and has been known as an accident black spot.

Main Street, Ravenfield, with Garden Lane to the right and Pingle Lane to the left. In the 1920s, Ravenfield was described as a pleasant and secluded village and parish. Thos Bolle Bosvile, of Ravenfield Park, was once Lord of the Manor and sole landowner.

The church of St James at Ravenfield, erected in 1756. A plain building of stone, the church consists of chancel, nave and tower. The church was restored in 1895 and afforded 140 sittings.

E.L.5 163-4. Victoria Park, Rawmarsh.

The former Victoria Park Hall/Rosehill Park Hall was converted in 1966, to a cafe and branch library on the ground floor and two flats on the first floor. The area of the whole parkland was noted at 34 acres and the land was purchased for £4,000 in 1900, being officially opened by W.H. Holland MP, on 27 May 1901. On 9 April 1973 a new building was erected in the Park at a cost of 6,000 for use by aged persons as a day centre and was furnished by with the aid of grants from the West Riding Social Services Committee to help form the basis of a meeting place for aged persons in the district.

E.L.5 163-3. Victoria Park, Rawmarsh.

The parish church of St Mary the Virgin is shown dominating the landscape from the top of Rawmarsh Hill. The church dates from 1838 when an earlier tower was increased in height and all the rest rebuilt. The architect was J.P. Pritchett. In 1869, the tower was rebuilt incorporating the features of the original Norman doorway. In 1894 further redevelopment took place, with vestry, organ chamber and north porch being added.

Another view of Rawmarsh with the council offices and library on the right. The *Rawmarsh Official Guide* of 1953 said the complimentary industries of steel and coal were the basis of working life in Rawmarsh. An approximate deviation of the name Rawmarsh is 'Red Marsh' possibly accounted for by the town's situation in the Permian system of red sandstone and marls which runs through this part of South Yorkshire.

One of the only examples discovered of Scrivens copying an engraving to make a postcard view, is of Roche Abbe around 1820. The area has been described as 'a pile of stately ruins - beautiful even in decay, which but faintly convey a slight idea of its former great extent, and splendour of structure.' With their usual eye for a perfect situation, the Cistercian Order of Monks founded a retreat at Roche, around the year 1150, and here in this beautiful rock-bound valley, with its rippling streams, their successive generations, for 400 years, exercised their various functions. In the early twentieth century the Abbey ruins were presented to the nation by the Earl of Scarbrough.

Roche Abbey, seen from a distance. In 1776 the Earl of Scarbrough commissioned noted landscape gardener Lancelot 'Capability' Brown to create a beauty spot from the ruinous area. This involved planting woodlands and setting lawns.

The Cottage, Roche Abbey.

Roche Abbey.

The stepping stones at Roche Abbey, featuring, it is believed, two of photographer Scrivens' daughters.

Two views of Sandbeck. The first recorded house at Sandbeck was built around 1626 by Sir Nicholas Saunderson. Sir Nicholas's family were succeeded by the Lumleys in 1724 when James Saunderson left Thomas Lumley his large estates in Lincolnshire and Yorkshire. Amongst these were houses at Sandbeck and Glentworth. Thomas Lumley was a younger son of the 1st Earl of Scarborough, becoming 3rd Earl of Scarborough, his elder brother predeceasing him. Plans survive from this time for remodelling the house but were never carried out, probably due to Thomas's lack of finances. Thomas died in 1752 and his son and heir married in the same year, to Barbara Savile living at Glentworth. In the following year, the couple engaged James Paine to produce plans for altering Glentworth, but these were never carried out. Preferring to live at Sandbeck, they then moved there. James Paine was first called to Sandbeck in 1757, making a number of drawings for a variety of the Earl's building plans. Eventually, Paine produced ideas to make alterations and additions to the old house. Then came a payment of £52 10s for 'preparing the several workmen's instructions by his Lordship and directing the building of the north and south ends and the intermediate part of the east front.' Incomplete records for the time introduce some doubt as to when the work was carried out, but it is thought to have taken place around 1760. Other records suggest that the house was remodelled rather than rebuilt.

95-1. South Anston.

A panoramic view from North Anston to South Anston prior to the construction of the A57 by-pass. William White in 1838 said Anston contains the well built and pleasant villages of North and South Anston situated on opposite acclivities of the fertile vale of a small rivulet which flows eastward to the Ryton, twelve miles east –south – east of Sheffield, six miles west of Worksop, in the heart of limestone district.

West Street, looking towards Sheffield Road, where the methodist chapel, built in 1871, can be seen in the distance. In 1934, this chapel was superseded by another, built on an adjacent site (Chapel Yard) in the memory of James Turner J.P. An alley way on the left, where the man and child are noticeable, leads to Maltkiln Yard. At the time the picture was taken J.W. Moor was the licensee of the Leeds Arms, on the right.

Sheffield Road, South Anston, showing the new methodist chapel on the right. Designed by B.D. Thompson of Worksop, it was erected in memory of James Turner and built in the Norman style of Southwell Minster.

West Street, South Anston, (from Sheffield Road) where a number of the buildings on both sides of the street have been demolished or drastically altered. Historically, South Anston was principally a farming community, though many hands were employed in related industries including quarrying for sand and stone. During 1846, South Anston methodists found accommodation in the Lodge Room over the stables of the Leeds Arms (on the left). Gardens of Remembrance now replace the three storey building on the right.

The church of St Margaret, Swinton, built in 1816, was destroyed by fire in March 1897, with the exception of the tower. It was rebuilt, partly from the remains of the old one, at a cost of over £6,000, and afforded 600 sittings. There is a memorial window to the Revd John Levett, vicar there from 1851-1895; the organ, provided at a cost of £680, was dedicated in January 1903.

Scene on the bowling green, Welfare Ground, Swinton.

Thrybergh Hall is a late Georgian castellated house, the front symmetrical with angle turrets and porch. In an article headed 'Thrybergh Park Estate - to be sold for building purposes,' the *Doncaster Chronicle* of 4 January 1929 recalled that the Hall was formerly the home of the Reresby family. 'The estate eventually came into the possession of the Fullerton family, and it has now been sold by J.S. Fullerton, a former master of the Badsworth Hunt.' The newspaper added that the Thrybergh estate included the mansion house, park, Rotherham golf course, five farms, several secondary residences, woodlands, twenty-three cottages, freehold ground rents and a large area of valuable building land ripe for development.

The Lodge, Thrybergh Hall.

E.L.S. 225-14. The Lodge, Thrybergh Hall.

E.L.S. 225-11. The Greenhouse, Thrybergh Hall.

The Greenhouse, Thrybergh Hall.

E.L.S.236-14. Reading Room, Treeton.

In his *Parish Study of Treeton* (1969) J.P. Dannatt says the village hall or 'Reading Room' serves many purposes, 'It is a small sub-library of the WRCC. It is also used for dancing classes, Treeton Horticultural Society meetings...'. Another recent one to which the Reading Room has been put, is a pre-school group.

L.S.236-17. The Rectory, Treeton.

The Rectory, Treeton. Until the arrival of the railways and associated coal mines, the life of Treeton village was strictly rural. From 1881 to 1891 the population tripled from 482 to 1301.

Wath Hall built in 1770, occupies the former site of a fourteenth century manor house. Its occupants have included William Kaye, James Barton (who used it as a boarding school), and Frederick Johnson, its last resident. On the left, in the above picture, is the memorial for the local brewer, Spedding Whitworth. In 1891, the hall was sold to Wath UDC for £2,500, becoming Wath Town Hall.

Scene in Wath High Street. The *Wath-upon-Dearne and District Almanack* of 1914 mentions that Wath's principal industries were the Manvers Main Collieries (Nos 1, 2 and 3 pits); the Wath Main (Nos 1 and 2 collieries) with the new coking plant; the Great Central Railway Company's new concentration yard; Messrs Chas Stanleys & Sons oil, manure, chemical and soap works; Whitworth, Son & Nephew's breweries and malt house; and the gas works. Occupation was also found for a considerable number of workers, by the local builders, contractors, farmers etc. The population in 1912 was 12,392. Plans were mooted for a tramway system serving Wath before the First World War, but the construction of a route through the town did not begin until 1923.

The sinking of Manvers in 1870, and Wath Main, beginning in 1875, made mining the principal source of employment in the area for many years.

Doncaster Road, Wath with Nash Row and the Manvers Main Colliery in the distance. The Dearne & Dove Canal, completed in 1797, is on the right. Manchester House (a drapery store) and Common Lane, are on the left. The canal was a very profitable investment to its shareholders, being the main outlet for the coal trade before the coming of the railways.

High Street, Wath, with the Co-op on the right.

Panoramic view of the Hump, Wath Sidings.

View of Wath Church. The church of All Saints is an ancient building of stone in the Norman and Early English styles, and consists of chancel, nave, aisles, south porch and tower with spire. A stained glass, east window was given by the late Miss Alice Otter in 1851, and at the restoration of the church in 1868 the two centre lancet lights of the north window were filled with stained glass by Messrs John and William Johnson as a memorial to Samuel Johnson and Ann, his wife. There were sittings for 517 persons, the register dating from 1598.

High Street looking west. On the right is the Lewis Watson's business premises. Adjacent is the London, City and Midland Bank.

Montgomery Road, Wath. The poet James Montgomery arrived in Wath as a youth of seventeen in 1789, and for a time lived and worked in a house/shop in the High Street.

A scene in Melton Road, Wath.

View of Burman Road, Wath. Wath was once described as a township, and was an extensive parish and town situated on a pleasant acclivity near the Dearne and Dove canal with stations on the Wath and Kirk Smeaton branch of the Hull and Barnsley railway, on the South Yorkshire branch of the Great Central railway and on the main line of the Midland railway. Earl Fitzwilliam was formerly Lord of the Manor.

Looking along Cross Street, Wath.

Unveiling the Wath War Memorial.

The public baths at Wath were opened in 1911 by the Urban District Council at a cost of £2,500.

Wharncliffe Crescent, Wath.

Doncaster Road, Wath.

E.L.S. 29-63. Manvers Main Colliery, Wath.

After conducting sinking operations, which extended over a period of 15 months at the new shaft at Manvers Main Colliery, near Wath, coal was reached at eleven o'clock in the morning on Monday 15 April 1901. The hoisting of a small flag on the top of the winding gear was the outward visible token of this interesting fact. The new shaft was close to Manvers Main No.1 pit, being separated on the surface only by the Great Central Railway running from Mexborough to Barnsley. The coal reached was part of what was known as the Parkgate seam, found at a depth of 550 yards. Eighty men were employed in shifts in the sinking of the shaft and not one injury was suffered by a workman. Unlike most other collieries, Manvers was not the centre of one village inhabited chiefly by its employees. The workmen lived principally at Wath, Swinton and Mexborough, with a few at Bolton, Adwick and Barnburgh.

E.L.S. 29-12. WHARNCLIFFE CRESENT, WATH.

Wharncliffe Crescent, Wath

Church House, Wath.

Looking along Doncaster Road, Wath.

Wentworth has a long association with the Fitzwilliam family. The Wentworth Holy Trinity Church, was designed by J.L. Pearson, and built between 1873 and 1877 at a cost of around £25,000. It was erected in the memory of the parents of William, the 6th Earl of Fitzwilliam, and in that of his wife Harriet, the Countess Fitzwilliam. Many items in the church commemorate the Fitzwilliam family. Several Earls and Countess Fitzwilliams are buried in a private cemetery at the rear of the church.

Wentworth tenants present a cup to the Earl and Countess Fitzwilliam at the christening of Earl Fitzwilliam's heir at Wentworth on 11 February 1911.

The Earl and Countess Fitzwilliam, starting on a drive round the park, at the christening of Earl Fitzwilliam's heir.

The miners' representatives present a cup to the Earl and Countess Fitzwilliam at the christening of Earl Fitzwilliam's heir.

E.L.S.165-20. Wentworth Woodhouse From The Gardens.

Wentworth Woodhouse, often called the most extraordinary house in England, has the longest facade – 606 feet – of any private house in the country. Thomas Watson Wentworth, 1st Earl and Marquess of Rockingham began building the house in 1724. The interior, equally as remarkable as the exterior, covers most of the styles of the eighteenth century. The view above shows the Garden Front, or more commonly known as the Back Front.

E.L.S.165-23. Wentworth Woodhouse.

Greasbrough Lodge, Wentworth Park.

In the gardens, Wentworth Woodhouse.

His First "Meet." —
E.L.S.3. Viscount Milton With The Hounds At Wentworth Woodhouse, Nov. 7, 1913.

The picture shows Peter Fitzwilliam being introduced to hunting. The groom in attendance is a Mr Dawes. There were Wentworths at Wentworth from the thirteenth century, right up until 1695. The estate passed to the Watson family in that year and then to the 1st Marquis of Rockingham in 1746. The 2nd Marquis died in 1782, and the estate passed to the 4th Earl Fitzwilliam. The estate then remained with the Fitzwilliams until the 10th Earl died in 1979. Thereafter, there being no heir, the estate was divided.

Wentworth.   Scriven

The Mechanic's Institute, built in 1835, and described as 'an extraordinary Gothic exercise with corner turrets, [once] provided a Christian men's working club.' At one time it was said to contain a library of 3,500 volumes.

Two views of Wentworth Woodhouse village, said to be an exceptional and fascinating agricultural estate village, in the small rural enclave of South Yorkshire, beleaguered on all sides by the encroaching sprawl of Rotherham, Sheffield and Barnsley, and only a few miles east of the M1. It is the central estate village of the old Fitzwilliam estate, once an outstanding example of a fully orchestrated village, developed and maintained by the estate for the occupation of its workers over centuries. The houses and cottages in the estate village are built of soft, local sandstone, with massive, graded stone tiles.

E.L.S. 165-112. The Square, Wentworth.

Paradise square, formerly a farm with cottages and outbuildings placed around the farmyard. The picture was taken in front of the farmhouse, looking towards the main street.

E.L.S. 165-104. Wentworth.

Main Street, Wentworth Woodhouse. The road was macadamised around 1914.

Within the Wentworth Woodhouse estate are a number of follies/monuments, built during the eighteenth century, satisfying a contemporary craze for that type of feature. These include Hoober Stand, Keppel's Column, the Needle's Eye and the Mausoleum. The latter was designed by John Carr, and built in 1788 by the 4th Earl of Fitzwilliam, in memory of his uncle the 2nd Marquis of Rockingham, who was twice Prime Minister. The statue of the 2nd Marquis of Rockingham inside the mausoleum is by Nollekens.

E.L.S. 165-37. The Mausoleum, Wentworth Park.

E.L.S. 165-115. The Needle's Eye, Wentworth.

Wentworth is said to have some of the best follies in the country. The Needle's Eye, dating from 1780, and lying at the edge of Lee Wood, is the smallest of the four major monuments, and its origins still baffle historians.

69

Hoober Stand, a triangular and tapering structure with a hexagonal lantern, extending 518 feet above sea level, was supposedly built in 1748 to commemorate the quelling of the Jacobite Rebellion in 1745. Others believe its construction was to show Lord Melton's public gratitude for his elevation to the position of Marquis of Rockingham by George II.

Fitzwilliam Arms public house, Wentworth, which, allegedly, takes its name from the Marquess of Rockingham in the eighteenth century.

The Round House, in Clayfields Lane, Wentworth, has also been known as the 'Saxon Tower.' It may have originally been a working windmill and was converted to a dwelling in the early nineteenth century.

The Mausoleum Lodge, Wentworth Park.

E.L.S. 165-129. The Stables, Wentworth Woodhouse.

The Stable Block is Paladian in style, and dates from 1768, being the work of John Carr. At one time it could accommodate 84 horses.

E.L.S. 165-90. The Riding School, Wentworth Woodhouse.

The Riding School, Wentworth.

Wentworth's old church was originally a chapel-of-ease. Large scale alterations and rebuilding took place in 1485 and 1684. In the mid-1920s, the chancel and north chapel were restored by the 7th Earl of Fitzwilliam. The main south porch, the tower and parts of the walls remain. In more recent times, under the ownership of the Redundant Churches Trust, the church was extensively restored. There are some impressive family monuments inside the church, including a floor brass, Elizabethan tomb effigies and wall monuments.

E. L. S. 165-72. Wentworth Old Church.

E. L. S. 165-92. The Doric Lodge, Wentworth Park.

The Doric Lodge, Wentworth Park, was probably designed by Pritchett & Watson, and built in the early nineteeth century. It resembles a Tetra-style Greek Doric Temple.

Two views of Whiston, both taken from impressive vantage points, with the Methodist church featuring prominently. It was built in 1866, and replaced an earlier chapel erected in 1822. Prior to this time, the Wesleyans held meetings, between 1771-1822, in Stanley Cottage on Hollowgate. In 1874 the Parish clock was placed in the chapel tower, paid for by public subscriptions. Eleanor Kimber in *Youthful Memories,* undated, states, 'Sunday at Chapel was a very full day for some of us. An early prayer meeting, asking for a spiritual blessing on the day's service, followed by Sunday School at 9.30 am and the service at 10.00 am. The family from the manor house filled the top pew every Sunday morning, and a full row of well-dressed ladies and gentlemen walked up the street after service - no cars then to obstruct pedestrians as they took a leisurely walk.' The old wooden spire was replaced with the concrete spire in 1949 at a cost of £290. The contractors for the work were Messrs Andrews, Baldwin & Co.

E.L.S. 224-3. *Whiston Church And Rectory.*

Whiston Church and Rectory. The *Star* of 7 May 1959 said Whiston is a village with a split personality. To the Rotherham side, and on the hills, there are new estates. Below, nestling in a hollow, is one of the best examples of an English village. It consists mainly of old stone cottages, some of them in terraces on the hill, and between which run little paths and steps. *Whiston Parish Church Visitor's Guide* states that for over 800 years the parish church of St Mary Magdalene has stood above the village. The reason for the church's position above and outside the settlement is unclear. It is tempting to speculate that the village may have originally clustered around the church but later migrated into the valley where water was more readily available. An alternative thesis might be that the church occupied a site of pre-Christian religious significance.

E.L.S. 224-8. *The Stocks, Whiston.*

Standing north of the lych gate are the village stocks, which as can be seen, could accommodate three people. One of the stone posts bears the date 1768.

Whiston church of St Mary Magdalene is an edifice in the Norman and Late Decorative styles. It was restored and partly rebuilt under the direction of Sir Gilbert Scott at a cost of around £8,000, towards which Lady Charlotte Howard (d.1886) made a donation of £5,000 in memory of her brother the Revd William Howard, rector there in 1841. The interior contains several stained windows, including one added in 1890 to Henry, 2nd Earl of Effingham (d. 5 Feb. 1889) and another one of 1891 commemorating the Deakin family. The register dates from 1594.

Whiston has been described as a village built on several levels, the main part being like a great cleft in the surrounding countryside, but at both ends it levels out and joins with the surrounding landscape.

Hell Hole, Whiston meadows.

A church at Wickersley was built from a very early period. The later Early English church, was said to have had a chancel with a Lady Chapel and one belonging to the Lord of Wyckersley. And, although still in good condition it was taken down, with the exception of the tower, in 1834. The present church of St Albans is a building of stone in the Gothic style, consisting of chancel, erected in 1886 at a cost of about £300, nave and an embattled tower. The reredos was erected in 1890 as a memorial to the late William Aldam, Lord of the Manor, who died in 1890. The register dates from 1540 and a list of rectors extends back to 1240.

The White Swan inn, Wickersley, when Fred Longden was the licensee. Also to be seen in the distance is the Masons Arms. William White in 1913 stated that the Parish is well-known for quarries of fine soft grit stone of which grit stones were made for the Sheffield grinders. The population in 1911, around the time these Wickersley pictures were taken, was 953.

The Bramley and Wickersley School was built in 1909 to serve both the parishes of Bramley and Wickersley.

A 'receiving house' was opened in Wickersley in 1847-1848, receiving letters from and for a mail cart service, operating between Rotherham and Bawtry. In 1860 the 'receiving house' was upgraded to a 'Post Office', with Sarah Unwin being appointed as Postmistress at £2 a quarter. She also 'doubled' as the letter carrier, delivering mail to Bramley, Flanderwell, Hellaby and Brecks.

The rectory at Wickersley was demolished in 1955.

View of Bawtry Road, Wickersley. For most of the area's early history, farming was the dominant influence. But from the early seventeenth century, quarrying was an important village industry, becoming a major employer in the area. There was also a tannery attached to a local farm. In the years following the First World War, the population expanded to over 7,000; the development of Listerdale by Joseph Lister, in the 1930s, adding considerably to this.

Morthen Road, Wickersley.

Old houses, Morthen Road, Wickersley.

Around 1800, Robert Wylde Moult resided at Wickersley Grange when it was a one-storeyed building with a thatched roof. Moult left the estate to his nephew, a Mr Aldred, with the proviso that the house should not be altered. In spite of this, the Grange was demolished and rebuilt afterwards in a Georgian style.

View of Nether Moor, Wickersley.

Two
Rotherham
The Town

All Saints Square, which during the 1930s, became the main town centre terminus for motorbuses and trolleybuses.

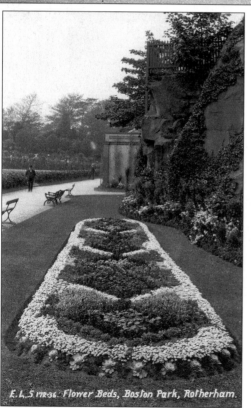

E.L.S. 172-36. Flower Beds, Boston Park, Rotherham.

Boston Castle, a small square building with battlements, was erected in 1775 by the 4th Earl of Effingham, who supported the American cause in the War of Independence. Until 1872, Boston Wood was just woodland and quarries worked by a Mr Birks. A little later, Rotherham Corporation made an arrangement with the Effinghams to lease the area and convert it to a park. The official opening took place on the centenary of the Declaration of Independence 4 July 1876. Thereafter thousands of people from all around the district made their way to this 'lung of Rotherham.' It was said that the flower beds were once the envy of the whole of Yorkshire, and many compliments were paid to the park keeper, Henry Albiston, for his floral displays. When the lease expired, the Corporation purchased the park from the Earl of Effingham.

The castle was allegedly built as a shooting lodge/place from which to admire the view from that point. During 1876, it was derisively noted in the *Rotherham Advertiser* as a 'castellated pigeon cote.' Tea drinking was said to have been forbidden at the castle's house warming.

Just after one o'clock 4 July 1886, the Volunteer Brass Band led a carriage procession of both local and visiting guests through the town to the Park where the Mayor and Mayoress of Rotherham were waiting to greet them. A procession made up of guests and members of the Town Council, and led by the band and Ald. John Guest as commanding officer, made a circuit of the Park. While this was going on, carriages were plying to and from Rotherham bringing crowds of visitors to the Park for the first time. By the time the civic party returned to the castle, a large gathering had formed in a circle in front of the castle. Ald. Guest then formally handed over the park and castle to the Mayor, and Ald. B.E.C. Chambers 'for the free use of the public.

A feature of Boston Park is the doorway from Jesus College founded by Thomas Rotherham in 1483.

E.L.5. 172-9. Boston Park, Roth

Scene in Boston Park.

Bridgegate is seen in these two views before the thoroughfare was widened during the 1920s. The (false) half-timbered building on the left, (bottom picture), is the Turf Tavern, which took its name in 1870, previously being known, from at least 1822, as the Boot and Shoe. The Turf closed in 1915 and was subsequently demolished in the redevelopment. New premises were later opened in Corporation Street.

A later view of Bridgegate, facing the gasworks offices, seen in the distance on Frederick Street. Barclays Bank and the White Hart are featured on the left; the Sheffield House is on the right.

Bridgegate looking towards All Saints Church, rising magnificently in the background. A lorry belonging to chemist H. Davy may be seen off-centre to the left. Amongst the properties on the right are Limbach's and the Angel Hotel. The latter was originally titled the Bull, the name change occurring during the late eighteenth century. The premises were rebuilt in 1915 during the redevelopment of Bridgegate, H.L. Taconand & Son providing the designs. The motor vehicle of photographer Scrivens is included in the composition, off-centre to the right.

The Bridge Inn, in both these pictures, was built around 1778. The building in the picture below was demolished during the late 1920s, a new pub being built in 1933. The delay in rebuilding was caused by the construction of a new bridge, needed because the increase of traffic was too much for the ancient bridge to endure. Strengthening was carried out in the early 1920s, but a new bridge was completed in 1930. Building the new bridge and the preservation of the old one was carried out by the former Borough Engineer, Maj. Vincent Turner. The work on the old bridge was supervised by W. Bond, of HM Office of Works (Ancient Monuments). An opening ceremony was performed on 28 April 1930 by Minister of Transport, Herbert Morrison, in the presence of the Mayor Ald. E. Cruikshanks, members of the Corporation, the Feoffees of the Common Lands and numerous other local dignitaries.

E.L.S. 172-123. *Chapel On The Bridge, Rotherham.*

The chapel on the bridge, featured in both pictures, dates from around 1483, and part of the cost of construction is believed to have been defrayed by Thomas Rotherham, Archbishop of York. For a period between 1779 - 1826 it was used as a prison, with a cell in the crypt. During its life-span it has also been used as an alms house, a dwelling, and tobacconist's shop. Since 1924, when it was converted again for religious use, services have been held there.

E.L.S. 172-122. *Chapel On The Bridge, Rotherham.*

Two close-up views of the chapel on the bridge, a subject which obviously appealed to Scrivens. There are only four surviving bridges, or chantry chapels in England, two of which are in Yorkshire, one at Wakefield, the other in Rotherham.

A view along Broom Road..

Another view of the chapel on the bridge. At one time it was said that a light was lit in the chapel every night to guide travellers into Rotherham. The chapel might also have been used in the past as a place to house people suspected of having the plague.

All Saints Parish Church with the 180ft spire clearly in evidence. A church had existed on the site from around AD 937. The present church dates from the thirteenth century, though has undergone many changes during the intervening years, not least the restorations of 1873-1875. Part of the market can be seen in the foreground.

Interior view of All Saints Church.

The altar, All Saints Church.

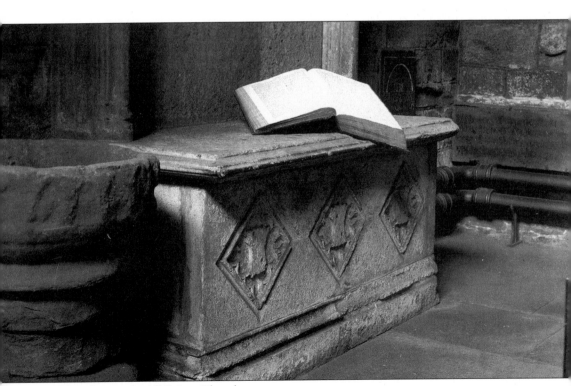

The altar tomb, All Saints Church.

The font, All Saints Church.

E L 5 172-152. The Screen. Rotherham Church

The screen, All Saints Church.

Church Street with Imperial Buildings on the left. This latter structure was erected by
Rotherham Corporation in 1906-1907 on the site of the old meat shambles. It originally
consisted of 18 shops facing Market Street, High Street and Church Street, with meat shops in
the interior and offices on the upper floors.

Church Street, where the traders at this time were Albert Upstone, seedsman; Alfred France,
butcher; Woodhead Bros, electrical engineers; Henry Gorrill, grocer; John D. Eaton,
pawnbroker; Harold Maxfield, toy dealer; and the Singer Sewing Machine Co. Ltd.

Church Street, showing Imperial Buildings in the distance.

Clifton Park was purchased by Rotherham Corporation in 1891. Following improvements, it was opened to the public by the Prince of Wales (later King Edward VII and Queen Alexandra) on 25 June of that year. Clifton House, built by Joshua Walker (1750-1815) during the 1780s and later occupied by William Owen, was opened as a museum in 1893. Local societies and individuals contributed items to the displays and a Mr Key of the Victoria & Albert Museum superintended the placing of items in the various cases. It was the intention that the museum would become 'a centre of education and recreation combined' for the people of Rotherham.

E.L.S.172-12. Birdcage Lodge, Clifton Park, Rotherham.

The lodge at the Doncaster Road entrance to the park is thought to have been built in the 1830s. Shown on the 1851 OS map as Clifton Lodge, it was known locally as 'Birdcage Lodge,' probably because a narrow road opposite was named Birdcage Lane. Before being demolished in 1946, it was used as a house by park keepers and gardeners.

S.172-54. The Lake, Clifton Park, Rotherham.

Clifton Park was intended to serve the needs of the growing population settling in the Eastwood area. Initially, £500 was spent on improvements. The opening ceremony was attended by thousands, and was celebrated with fire works, bands, coconut shies and dancing. The high spot of the afternoon was a balloon ascent by Capt. Whelan of Huddersfield, which nearly ended in disaster when Cllr Thomas became entangled with the ropes and was almost carried off hanging upside down by the legs. Fortunately, he managed to disentangle himself.

E.L.S. 172-41. Entrance, Clifton Park, Rotherham.

The main entrance to the park at the Clifton Lane/Doncaster Road corner was improved around 1900, with the erection of massive pillars and cast-iron gates. However, the gates were removed during the Second World War and the entrance remodelled in subsequent years.

172-42. War Memorial, Clifton Park, Rotherham.

The Clifton Park cenotaph was unveiled in November 1922.

Swans at Clifton Park. In *Clifton House and Park* (1992) it is said that the 'old fish pond became a popular ornamental lake, with ducks and wild fowl, but was later considered to be insanitary, and was replaced in 1939 by a children's paddling pool.'

Clifton Park – note the tank in the distance.

An original cast-iron bandstand survived until 1919, when it was transferred to Ferham Park. The base was occupied by a First World War tank until 1927. A new bandstand was erected in 1928, to be replaced by another, opened by HM Queen Elizabeth II in 1991, to commemorate the Park's centenary.

Near the bandstand was a lawn and a picnic area. After the Second World War, brass bands played dance music in the bandstand on Sunday nights. Bands such as the Habershon Brass Band, the Silverwood Colliery Band and the Salvation Army Band gave concerts for charity.

Judging by the number of pictures Scrivens took of the College Square area of Rotherham, he obviously liked this location. Here we see College Square, with College Street or Jesus Gate to the left and Effingham Street to the right. Note the children on a charabanc in the foreground and Sheffield Corporation tramways vehicle No. 72 to the right. Tram services were operated between Sheffield and Rotherham by the Corporations of both these areas. During the mid-1920s, the journey by tram between Rotherham and Sheffield (about six miles), took around thirty-five minutes. The single fare was 4d for an adult and 1½ d for a child. The building just hidden by the tram was built in 1828 to house the Rotherham dispensary. To the left of this is the route to Church Steps Yard. The photograph was taken from outside the Court House.

A view of College Square (looking down Effingham Street towards Howard Street) where Sheffield, Rotherham, and Mexborough & Swinton trams can be seen. South Yorkshire's tramway systems were laid to the standard gauge of 4ft 8½ in. At one time it was possible to travel by tram from Barnsley, via the Dearne Valley, Swinton and Rotherham, to Sheffield.

To the left is the Falstaff Inn, dating back to at least 1869. The inn closed in 1993, the building becoming a branch of the Bradford & Bingley Building Society.

College Square with part of the College Inn visible on the right.

College Square where several business premises are on view including those of Block & Cleaver, butchers (in Compton House); Morgan & Co; and the Sheffield & Hallamshire Bank.

Another view of Compton House (left) and College Square.

College Square and Effingham Street, with the court house (on the right), built in 1828, and survived until the early part of the twentieth century. Three Rotherham trams are on view in this picture. Under the Rotherham Corporation Act of 1900, Rotherham obtained powers to operate and maintain tramways. The 'Electric Light and Tramways Committee,' was formed, and the powers obtained were implemented immediately. Operations commenced with the opening of two routes on 31 January 1903; College Square to Rawmarsh Road and Fitzwilliam Road. For the first 'official' year of tramcar operation, ending 31 March 1904, the receipts were £21,341.

College Square and Effingham Street. Note the charabanc on the right. St George's Hall, built in 1878, is the tall building in the distance on the right.

105

Looking along College Street, to College Square, with Scales & Sons premises on the left. In the distance is the Old College Inn, taking its name from the College of Jesus, founded by Archbishop Rotherham in 1842. Another pub, the Grapes, is on the right.

College Street, showing on the left, the premises of the South Yorkshire Wine & Spirit Co. Ltd, established 1790. At one time the company bottled Bass's Ales and Guinness's stout, and imported and bonded foreign wines and spirits, as well as being Havana cigar merchants.

College Street in the days of trolleybus operation. By powers obtained in the Rotherham Corporation Act 1911, Rotherham Transport Department was able to begin operating this type of transport, as well as motorbuses. By 1931, a start had been made on the conversion from tramcars to trolleybuses. The joint tramcar service operating with Sheffield Corporation continued up to December 1948, when it was changed to motorbus operation. However, trams still operated between Rotherham and the boundary at Templeborough, until it was converted to motorbus operation on 14 November 1949. So ended the tramcar era in Rotherham.

According to the Rotherham by-law and building plans 1897-1948, College Street saw much rebuilding and redevelopment work in the 1920s and 1930s. Plans were submitted by Burtons (1927), the Grand Clothing Hall (1922 and 1926), Marks and Spencers (1932) and Woolworths (1928).

E.L.S. 172 177. Coronation Fountain, Rotherham.

The Coronation Fountain, standing thirty-two foot high in Effingham Square. Businessman James Hastings offered to finance the project in November 1911. It was unveiled in a ceremony which took place around half past one in the afternoon, on 20 June, 1912. In 1962, it was moved for the redevelopment of the square. Later on in the decade, and following some restoration, it was replaced near its original site.

Two views of Doncaster Gate stretching towards the High Street/College Street/Wellgate junction. In the top picture Scales & Sons' premises have been replaced by Montagu Burton's building. The Wheatsheaf public house is off-centre to the right. The pub was rebuilt 1909-1910 when Howard Street was widened; closing June 1968. On the left is the Cinema House, the facade having a distinctive appearance. One of the buildings on the right was formerly used by the Conservative Club.

Effingham Square with Frederick Street to the right.

Effingham Square, with Whitworth, Son & Nephew's Grey Horse Inn on the left. The pub had held this name from 1872, previously being known, from 1862, as the Merry Heart. The premises closed on 25 February 1962, the licence transferred to the Tabard, Herringthorpe Valley Road, Herringthorpe.

Effingham Street looking in the direction of printer Henry Garnett & Co. whose business premises can be seen in the distance. In March 1929, the tramcar service between Effingham Street and Rotherham Bridge was converted to trolleybus operation, and in conjunction with the Mexborough & Swinton Tramways Co. a through service was introduced between Rotherham and Conisbrough.

Effingham Street, facing College Street and Davy's Cafe, in the days after the trams.

A busy day in Effingham Street, the traders including Walter Wragg, cycle dealer, and the Royal Tailoring Co. The picture was taken near the junction with Howard Street.

View along Frederick Street.

View along Fitzwilliam Road.

The Hippodrome (right) in Henry Street, built on the lines of the London West End Music Halls, opened on 3 August 1908. It was designed by Chadwick & Watson of Leeds, with a seating capacity of 2,500. Building work was carried out by J. Parkinson & Sons of Blackpool. The front facade is Italian renaissance in style and the two domes give balance and dignity to the elevation. The interior decorations were Georgian in character. In attendance at the opening performance was the Mayor Dr Lodge, the Town Clerk W. Board, and members of the local Corporation. The theatre closed on 2 July 1932, and was taken over by Rotherham Hippodrome Ltd, opening as a cinema on 17 October 1932. During 1959, the local Council revealed it was considering acquiring the cinema site to be incorporated in a new civic centre. The Hippodrome closed on 19 December 1959. The last films to be shown were *When the Devil Drives* and *Runaway Daughters*. The building on the left was formerly a Zion chapel, then became a picture house: the Electra and later the Pavilion.

The Grammar School's Old Boy's Association was responsible for the War Memorial scheme. The Memorial was unveiled by the Revd Hargreaves Heap on 19 February 1925 after a service in the Parish church, with the Archbishop of York preaching the sermon. The Memorial is in the form of a cross, designed from the period of the foundation of the school, the late fifteenth century. In the centre is a carved York rose, and the cross surmounts an octagonal column, standing upon an octagonal base. The names of the fifty-eight old boys and one master, who were killed in the War, are contained on bronze panels.

E.L.S 172-15. Grammar School, Rotherham.

The Grammar School was founded in 1482-1483 by Thomas de Rotherham, Archbishop of York, in grateful memory of the benefit he had derived from a teacher of grammar in his native town of Rotherham. The structure depicted here, erected in 1876 at a cost of £26,000, is in the Gothic style, with a central tower sixty feet high. In 1909, a scheme of extension and alteration was completed.

114

Chemist and druggist Humphrey Davy's premises are on the left in this view of High Street. He also had a business at 19 Bridgegate. He once boasted the 'best stock of nursing requirements, sick room appliances and special medicines.' At one time, the Maypole Dairy Co. Ltd was at No. 24, and grocer John Fawcet occupied Nos 18 and 20.

The building just off centre to the right, is occupied by the business premises of John Mason. In a *Rotherham and District Annual* it is stated, 'John Mason, jeweller of High Street, Rotherham, who also has a business at Barnsley, was born in 1831, and started in business in the town as a jeweller and clock maker - the traditional occupation of his ancestors for as many generations as can be traced - in 1854 opening his present establishment at the top of High Street in 1883. He was Mayor in 1888.' Tram No. 25 on the right is making its way to Kimberworth.

High Street, from Doncaster Gate. The building on the right, occupied by Scales & Salters' boot and shoe warehouse, took on its elaborate appearance in the 1870s, replacing an earlier building. Scales & Salter eventually became Scales & Son, surviving until the 1920s. Their premises were taken in the redevelopment of the area in the early 1930s, Montague Burton subsequently occupying the site. The bank on the left was built during the early 1890s as a new branch of the Sheffield and Rotherham bank.

The High Street/Moorgate Street/Church Street junction during the 1930s, traffic having built up to such an extent at this point that it was necessary to have a policeman on duty. In the distance the new building of Montague Burton can be seen.

High Street, with Corporation Street to the right and West Gate leading off to the left. The building in the centre belonged to the Masboro Equitable Pioneers Society Ltd.

A similar view to that on the previous page of the High Street, but this one was taken a little later. Scrivens had a habit of doing this. George Gummer in *Reminiscences of Rotherham* (1927) states, 'Previous to the erection of Imperial Buildings [on the left] great inconvenience was caused to vehicular and other traffic by the narrowness of that part of High Street. The new buildings were designed by Joseph Platt; the eventual cost of the entire scheme amounting to £19,283. On completion in 1908, the building was officially opened by Charles Stoddart.

Two photographs of the High Street, one being taken slightly in front of the other. The traders here once included Scales & Son (boot manufacturers); John Cox (tailor); Langton & Son (boot manufacturers) and Boots Ltd (chemists).

E.L.S. 172-119. *The Hospital, Rotherham.*

The first stone was laid for the Rotherham Hospital and Dispensary, standing in its own grounds of four acres in Doncaster Road, in 1870, by the Marquis of Ripon. The building was completed the following year at a cost of £10,000. A mortuary and disinfection ward were subsequently erected at the rear of the premises, at a cost of £300, and a new ward was built in 1886, at a cost of £1,000. A children's ward was added in 1897, at a cost of £800. The women's ward was enlarged in 1903. The old Dispensary which opened in 1806, was merged into the new Hospital and Dispensary in 1872. Two new wards, of twenty-two beds each, were completed in 1925 at a cost, including furniture, of about £14,000. Earl Fitzwilliam was the president, and the Mayor and the Greave of the Feoffees were vice presidents.

E.L.S. 172-169. *The Hospital, Rotherham.*

Keppel's Column, located on the southern periphery of Wentworth Park. It was erected in 1778 by the second Marquess of Rockingham, to commemorate the acquital of his friend Admiral Keppel.

Lindum Terrace, which was built during the 1860s. In a 1912 Rotherham and Sheffield Trade Directory, the Lindum Terrace residents at this time included: 'a teacher of music, goods agent, bank manager, head mistress, iron merchant and methodist minister.'

This post office was opened in Main Street in March 1907 by Sir Chas Stoddart. Prior to this the post office had been accommodated in the West Gate Station building since 1880.

Main Street, looking towards Kimberworth, where car No. 26 is pictured in a track loop. On the right are the public baths, free library, post office and stamp and tax offices. West Gate Station is to the left. The public library was opened in 1887 and destroyed by fire in July 1925. The public baths were also opened in 1887 at a cost of around £8,000, and in 1899 a new swimming bath was constructed. Due to fire damage in 1925, the baths were renovated and modernised at a cost of about £7,000.

E.L.S. 172-105. Main Street, Rotherham.

Two views of Masborough Street, not Main Street as titled by Scrivens. Orchard Street can be seen in the distance in the picture below.

S. 172-90. Main Street, Rotherham.

Market Place, with a rare view of the Tramway Department's track cleaner in operation.

View along Moorgate Street.

Moorgate, featuring the High House Hotel in the distance, (renamed High Bar in 1984). Paul Satterthwaite in *Rotherham Town Public Houses 1820 – 1990* mentions that the pub's name could be derived due to its location on fairly high ground at the top of Ship Hill. The Old Cross Keys is on the extreme left. All the property on the left, up to the High House Hotel, has since been demolished.

Moorgate, with All Saints Church in the distance. The buildings and occupants on the left included Rhodes Parker & Co. Solicitors, at No. 14; the West Riding and Borough Magistrates Clerks Office, at No. 16; the Vestry Offices/Hall, built 1894, at No. 18, and occupied by the County Court Offices, F. Parker Rhodes being the Registrar and High Bailiff.

View along Moorgate.

Errand boys in Moorgate. In the distance is the Unitarian Chapel (Church of Our Father), erected in 1879 at a cost of around £3,600. It is a building designed in the Early English style by E.M. Gibbs. The church closed in 1986 and is currently a mosque.

E.L.S. 172-165. St. Anne's Council School, Rotherham.

St Anne's Council School.

E.L.S. 172-117.   Rotherham.

South Terrace, Moorgate Street, with W. Crook's fruit stores in the distance.

View along Wellgate, looking towards College Street.

The town hall, situated in Frederick and Howard Streets, once contained the offices of the medical officer of health, and the police. Also houses the police courts, assembly rooms, mayors's and mayoress's parlours, members' rooms and committee rooms.

Wellgate, showing the Mail Coach public house in the distance on the left. Note the tramway passing loop in the foreground.

Westgate with Mrs Annie Bewley's newsagent and tobacconist shop on the left.